EXPERIMENTS WITH THE SUN AND THE MOON

A TRUE BOOK®

by

Salvatore Tocci

Children's Press®
A Division of Scholastic Inc.

New York Toronto London Auckland Sydney
Mexico City New Delhi Hong Kong
Danbury, Connecticut

Light from the moon brightens up the evening sky.

Reading Consultant
Susan Virgilio

Science Consultant
Robert Gardner

The photo on the cover shows an eclipse. The photo on the title page shows a sunrise.

The author and publisher are not responsible for injuries or accidents that occur during or from any experiments. Experiments should be conducted in the presence of or with the help of an adult. Any instructions of the experiments that require the use of sharp, hot, or other unsafe items should be conducted by or with the help of an adult.

Library of Congress Cataloging-in-Publication Data

Tocci, Salvatore.
    Experiments with the sun and the moon / Salvatore Tocci.
        p. cm. – (A true book)
    Summary: Projects and experiments explore scientific principles related to the sun and moon, particularly those which explain eclipses.
    Includes bibliographical references and index.
    ISBN 0-516-22605-3 (lib. bdg.)   0-516-27469-4 (pbk.)
    1. Astronomy—Experiments—Juvenile literature. 2. Sun—Juvenile literature. 3. Moon—Juvenile literature [1. Astronomy—Experiments. 2. Eclipses. 3. Sun. 4. Moon. 5. Experiments.] I. Title. II. Series.
QB46 .T63 2003
520'.78—dc21
                                                                                            2002001604

CHILDREN'S PRESS, AND A TRUE BOOK®, and associated logos are trademarks and or registered trademarks of Grolier Publishing Co., Inc. SCHOLASTIC and associated logos are trademarks and or registered trademarks of Scholastic Inc.
1 2 3 4 5 6 7 8 9 10 R 12 11 10 09 08 07 06 05 04 03

Contents

Where Did They Go?   5

How Can the Sun and the Moon
    Disappear?   10
    Experiment 1: Blocking the Sun
    Experiment 2: Hiding in the Shadows

What Makes a Full Moon?   18
    Experiment 3: Changing Its Shape
    Experiment 4: Passing Overhead
    Experiment 5: Circling Around

What Can a Shadow Tell You?   32
    Experiment 6: Telling the Time
    Experiment 7: Traveling in a Straight Line

Fun With the Sun and the Moon   40
    Experiment 8: Sending Messages

To Find Out More   44

Important Words   46

Index   47

Meet the Author   48

Where Did They Go?

Have you ever been outside on a sunny day when it suddenly started to get very dark? Most likely, a storm was approaching. Dark clouds suddenly may have rolled in and hidden the Sun. The clouds may then have moved on just as quickly as they came. The

Sun soon reappeared in the sky. The Sun's disappearance that day did not worry you. You knew that the clouds would eventually pass and that the Sun would shine again.

However, there are times when the Sun completely disappears when there isn't a cloud in the sky. For example, one day in 1995, the skies over Asia became very dark shortly after 8 A.M. A large dark spot had covered the Sun. Within minutes, millions of people went indoors, afraid that something terrible was about to happen. Millions of others felt they would be safe if they stayed in water up to their necks until the Sun returned.

Thousands of years ago, when something like this happened, people thought the Sun might never return. They believed that an evil spirit they called Rahu had eaten the Sun. They also

People once believed that gods controlled the Sun and the Moon. This drawing shows the Sun god being eaten by another god.

believed that Rahu could eat the Moon because they had seen the Moon disappear suddenly on clear nights.

8

To get Rahu to return the Sun and the Moon, people banged on metal and wooden objects. They thought the loud noises would scare off the evil spirit.

You don't have to make loud noises to get the Sun and the Moon back. All you have to do is carry out the experiments in this book to help you understand what happens when the Sun and the Moon suddenly disappear.

How Can the Sun and the Moon Disappear?

You know that Earth circles the Sun and that the Moon circles Earth. Every so often in their travels, Earth, the Moon, and the Sun are arranged in a straight line. When this happens, the Moon blocks out, or **eclipses**,

Notice how the Moon can come between Earth and the Sun.

the Sun. This called a **solar eclipse**. See how Earth, the Sun, and the Moon must be in just the right position for this to happen.

Blocking the Sun

You will need:
- modeling clay
- sharp pencil
- lamp with low-wattage bulb

Mold a small piece of the clay into a ball a little bigger than a grape. Stick the clay ball on the point of the pencil. Remove the lamp shade and turn on the light. Stand several feet away, facing the light. Hold the pencil straight out in front of your eyes. Close one eye.

Slowly move the clay ball toward your open eye. Notice that more and more of the lightbulb becomes hidden as you move the clay ball toward your eye. Can you hold the clay ball so that the central part of the lightbulb is hidden?

Do you see a ring of light
around the edge of the clay ball?

In this experiment, your eye acts as Earth. The
clay ball represents the Moon, while the lightbulb
serves as the Sun. When the Moon is in a certain
position, it blocks the light coming from the center

of the Sun. This leaves a thin ring of light around the Moon. This is called a partial solar eclipse because the Moon blocks only part of the Sun's light.

At times, the Moon is in a position that allows it to completely cover the Sun. When this happens, the Moon blocks all the Sun's light from

reaching Earth. This is called a total solar eclipse. If the Moon can block the Sun, can anything block the Moon?

14

Hiding in the Shadows

You will need:
- modeling clay
- two sharpened pencils
- 3-inch (8 centimeter) polystyrene ball
- measuring tape
- several books
- flashlight
- 2-inch (5 cm) polystyrene ball

Flatten a small piece of the clay. Push the eraser end of the pencil into the clay. Push the sharpened end of the pencil into the 3-inch (8 cm) polystyrene ball. Place the clay on the floor about 12 inches (30 cm) in front of a wall. The pencil should be standing straight up with the ball on top.

Stack some books 18 inches (46 cm) away from the pencil. Lay the flashlight on the books so that it faces the wall. Darken the room and turn on the flashlight. Be sure that the stack of books is high

enough that the light
shines directly on the ball. The ball should
cast a **shadow** on the wall.

Stick the point of the other pencil into the
2-inch (5-cm) ball. Hold the smaller ball about 2 inches
(5 cm) from the wall. Slowly move this ball through
the larger ball's shadow. Watch what happens to the
smaller ball as it passes through the shadow.

The flashlight represents the Sun. The larger ball
represents Earth, while the smaller one acts as the
Moon. As the Moon begins to pass

Earth blocks most of the Sun's light from reaching the Moon. As a result, only part of the Moon can be seen.

behind Earth, only part of it is hidden in the shadow. This is called a partial **lunar eclipse**. This happens when Earth keeps sunlight from reaching only a part of the Moon.

As the Moon continues to circle Earth, all of it becomes hidden in its shadow. This is called a total lunar eclipse. This happens when Earth blocks sunlight from reaching the entire Moon. Lunar eclipses happen only when the Moon is full.

17

What Makes a Full Moon?

On a clear night, you have probably searched the sky looking for the Moon. On some nights, you probably never found it, even though you could see plenty of stars. On many nights, you may have seen only part of the Moon. There were some nights,

Even though you may see lots of stars in the night sky, you still may not see the Moon.

however, when you saw the full Moon. Why does the shape of the Moon change?

Changing Its Shape

You will need:
- 3-inch (8 cm) polystyrene ball
- sharpened pencil
- tall lamp
- measuring tape
- helper

Stick the polystyrene ball on the point of the pencil. Place the lamp against a wall. Darken the room. Remove the lamp shade and turn on the lamp. Stand about 6 feet (2 meters) from the lamp. Look directly at the light. Ask someone to stand directly to your left while holding the polystyrene ball in front of his or her face. The light represents the Sun, the ball serves as the Moon, and you act as Earth.

Now make a quarter turn so that you are looking directly at the Moon. The Sun will be on your right. How does the Moon look?

The right half of the
Moon is bright, while
its left half is dark.
Have you ever seen
the Moon look like
this? This is called a
first quarter Moon.

The first quarter Moon
is usually seen between
noon and midnight.

Ask the person to move directly to your left. Turn to face the Moon. You should now see the whole Moon lit. This represents a full Moon. Once again, have the person move toward your left. How does the Moon look when you turn to face it? The right half of the Moon is dark, while the left half is lit by the Sun. This is called a third quarter Moon.

Finally, ask the person to stand directly between you and the lamp. Turn to face the Moon. In this position, the Moon is completely dark. The lighted side faces toward the Sun. This is called a new Moon.

Have you ever heard the expression "Once in a **blue Moon**"? Sometimes a full moon appears twice in the same month. When this happens, the second full Moon is called a blue Moon.

The time between one full Moon and the next is about twenty-nine days. During that time, you may see all these stages of the Moon. However, you need less than one day to find out what kind of path the Sun takes as it travels through the sky.

Passing Overhead

You will need:
- kitchen strainer
- clear plastic wrap
- white cardboard
- marker
- tape
- small rocks or large stones

Cover the strainer snugly with clear plastic wrap. Place the strainer with the open side facing down on the cardboard. Trace the outline of the strainer on the cardboard. Remove the strainer from the cardboard. Use the marker to make a dot in the center of the circle you drew. Then replace the strainer to its original position on the cardboard. Use tape to keep the strainer in place. Now all you need is a sunny day.

Shortly after sunrise, take the cardboard and strainer outside. Set them in a spot where they will be in the sun-

light all day. Place several small rocks on the cardboard so that it does not move. Place the tip of

The strainer represents half of Earth.

the marker on the plastic so that its shadow falls on the dot you drew in the center of the circle. Mark this point on the plastic with a dot. This dot marks the Sun's position at that time of the day.

Continue to mark the Sun's position throughout the day. When you are finished, use the marker to connect the dots you made on the plastic. This line represents the Sun's path through the sky that day.

Make sure that the shadow of the marker's tip falls directly on the dot you placed in the center.

Repeat this experiment at different times of the year. Be sure to place the strainer in the same spot every time. Does the Sun always pass overhead in the same path as Earth circles around it?

People once believed that the Sun circled Earth because they saw the Sun move across the sky. In the early 1500s, Nicolaus Copernicus, a Polish scientist, was the first to say that Earth actually orbits the Sun.

Copernicus said that all six of the planets known at the time orbited the Sun in perfect circles. Scientists later discovered that the planets do not orbit the Sun in perfect circles. What kind of path does Earth follow as it travels around the Sun?

Circling Around

You will need:
- marker
- sheet of cardboard
- ruler
- sharpened pencil
- two metal fasteners
- scissors
- string

Use the marker to make a dot in the center of the cardboard. This dot represents the Sun. Place another dot 2 inches (5 cm) away from the first dot. Use the pencil point to make a tiny hole through each dot. Then push a fastener through each hole. Open the flaps so that the fasteners stay in place.

Cut an 8-inch (20-cm) piece of string. Tie the ends

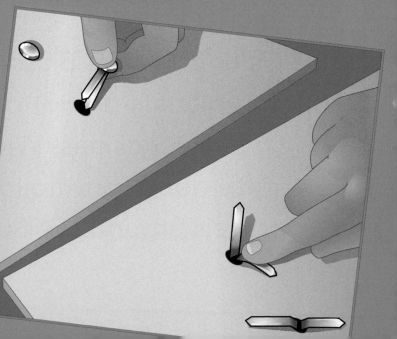

The path you trace is like the one that Earth takes as it travels around the Sun.

together to make a loop. Place the loop around the fasteners. Place the tip of the marker inside the loop. Pull the string so that it is fully stretched. Move the marker around the cardboard while pulling gently on the string. Remove the string and fasteners from the cardboard. What kind of shape did you draw?

The tip of the marker represents Earth as it circles the Sun. From the shape you drew, you can see that Earth does not make a circle as it travels around the Sun. It follows a path called an **ellipse**.

Like Earth, the other planets also follow an elliptical path as they travel around the Sun. The paths they follow, especially Earth's, are not as stretched out as the one you drew.

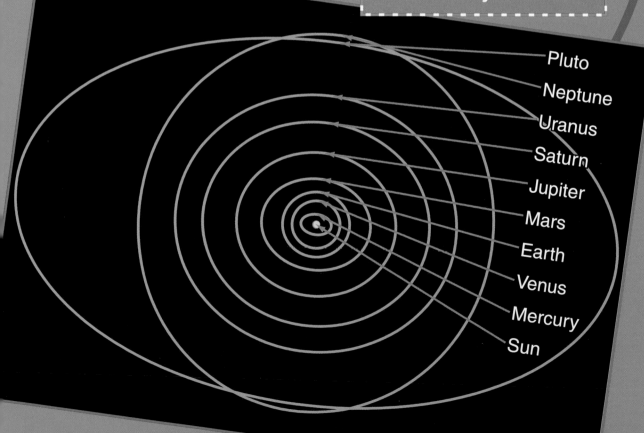

Pluto
Neptune
Uranus
Saturn
Jupiter
Mars
Earth
Venus
Mercury
Sun

Earth takes about 365 days to orbit the Sun, traveling at about 67,000 miles (108,000 kilometers) per hour. While it orbits the Sun, Earth is also spinning around. It takes twenty-four hours to make one complete spin. Only about half of the Earth faces the Sun at any one time because it is spinning. If you happen to be in a spot on Earth where the Sun is shining, you can see your shadow.

What Can a Shadow Tell You?

A shadow is made when an object blocks light. When light cannot pass through an object, the space behind the object is dark. This dark area is called a shadow. Shadows are made whenever the Sun is shining. Before there were

The shadows cast by a sundial were used to tell time even after clocks were invented.

clocks, people used the shadows made by the Sun to tell the time.

Experiment 6

Telling the Time

You will need:
- adult helper
- tape
- large square piece of white cardboard
- wooden board slightly larger than the cardboard
- ruler
- hammer
- long finishing nail
- pencil
- compass
- watch

Tape the cardboard to the wooden board. Ask an adult to hammer the nail through the cardboard and into the wood. The nail should be near the middle of one end, about 2 inches (5 cm) from the edge. Use the ruler to draw a straight line from the nail to the edge of the cardboard.

On the next sunny day, take the board outside as early as possible. Use the compass to place the board so that the line you drew points directly south. Check your watch for the time. Draw a line on the cardboard that follows the nail's shadow. Write the time of day on the line. Every hour, draw a line for as long as the Sun casts a shadow on the cardboard.

On the next sunny day, place the board in the same spot. Can you tell the time by looking at the nail's shadow? Experiment to see how long your "shadow" clock keeps the right time. For example, does your clock still give the same time one week later? One month later? What else can you learn about looking at a shadow made by the Sun?

Noon

11 a.m.

10 a.m.

1 p.m.

9 a.m.

2 p.m.

8 a.m.

3 p.m.

7 a.m.

3 4

N
W E
S

Be sure to mark each line with the time you drew it on the cardboard.

Traveling in a Straight Line

You will need:
- adult helper
- ruler
- pencil
- sheet of white card-board about 12 inches (30 cm) on each side
- tape
- wooden board about 12 inches (30 cm) on each side
- hammer
- six finishing nails
- lightbulb with a straight filament

Use the ruler and pencil to mark six points in the middle of the cardboard near the edge, 0.5 inches (1 cm) apart. Tape the cardboard to the wooden board. Ask an adult to hammer a nail into each point. Hold the edge of the board with the nails near the lightbulb. Hold the board so that the end of the lightbulb filament is pointing straight at the nails. Darken the room and turn on the light.

36

Look at the shadow lines made by the nails. Do you see that the lines spread out, just as your fingers do when you spread them?

Slowly move the board away from the light. What happens to the shadow lines? Do you see them getting straighter as you move the board? Take the board outside on a sunny day. Set it on the ground so that the sunlight casts the nails' shadows on the cardboard. How do the shadow lines look?

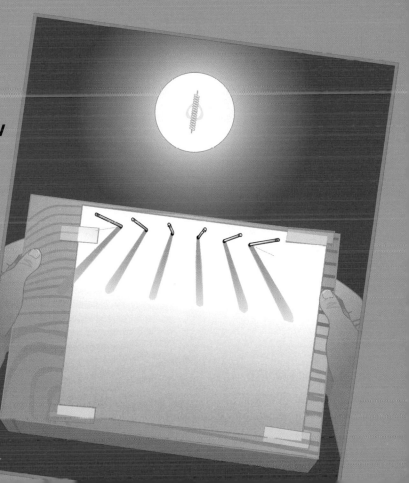

Hold the edge of the board with the nails so that it points straight at the end of the filament in the lightbulb.

As light leaves the bulb or the Sun, its rays spread out in all directions. This is why the shadow lines made by the lightbulb spread out when you hold the board close to the bulb. But as you get farther and farther away from the light source, the light rays spread out less and less. This is why the shadow lines get straighter as you move the board away from the lightbulb.

The Sun is 93 million miles (150 million km) from Earth. Because of this great distance, the light rays from the Sun are almost **parallel** when they reach Earth.

Because they travel so far in space, light rays from the Sun are almost parallel when they reach Earth.

Earth travels around the Sun in an elliptical orbit once every 365 days. The Moon travels around Earth in an elliptical orbit once every twenty-nine days. Sometimes during their travels, the Moon may come between Earth and the Sun. By blocking the Sun, the Moon causes a solar eclipse. At other times, Earth may come between the Sun and the Moon. By blocking the Sun, Earth may cause a lunar eclipse. Both the Sun and the Moon may disappear for a short time, but they always come back. Rahu does not eat them.

Fun With the Sun and the Moon

Now that you have learned some things about the Sun and the Moon, here is a fun experiment for you to try. See how you can use sunlight and moonlight to send secret messages to someone day and night. You will need both a sunny day and a night with a bright, full Moon.

Experiment 8

💡

Sending Messages

You will need:
- a helper
- two mirrors
- two pencils
- two pads of paper

Give one mirror to a friend or family member. Keep the other mirror for yourself. The two of you should try to get as far apart as possible. Have the sunlight reflect off each mirror so that it can be seen by the other person. Use Morse code to send one another messages. Send a brief flash of light for a dot and a longer flash for a dash.

If possible, stand on two hills that are some distance away from each other.

Practice by sending each other the Morse code for Sun and Moon. Write down each letter as it is sent.

Try sending a message at night by using the mirrors to reflect moonlight. Moonlight is actually sunlight that bounces off the Moon and travels to Earth.

Morse Code

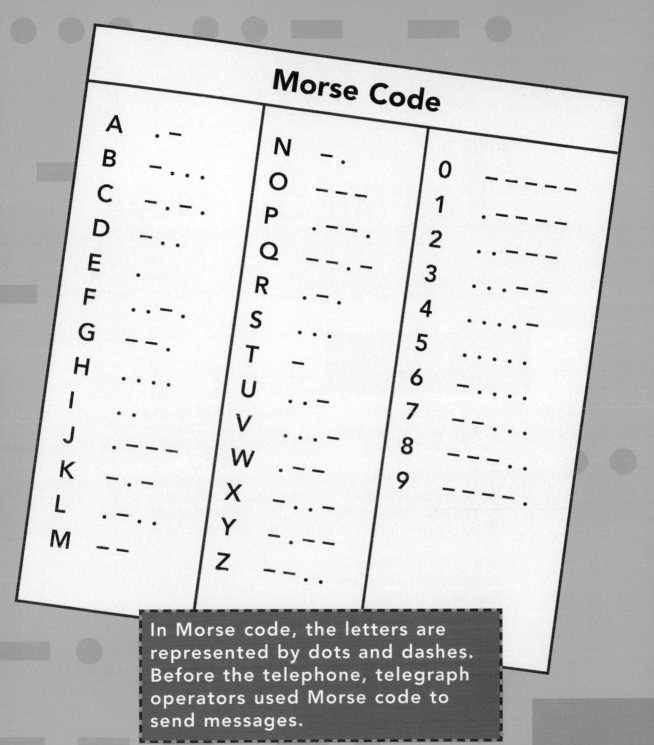

A	.-	N	-.
B	-...	O	---
C	-.-.	P	.--.
D	-..	Q	--.-
E	.	R	.-.
F	..-.	S	...
G	--.	T	-
H	....	U	..-
I	..	V	...-
J	.---	W	.--
K	-.-	X	-..-
L	.-..	Y	-.--
M	--	Z	--..

0	-----
1	.----
2	..---
3	...--
4	....-
5	.....
6	-....
7	--...
8	---..
9	----.

In Morse code, the letters are represented by dots and dashes. Before the telephone, telegraph operators used Morse code to send messages.

To Find Out More

If you would like to learn more about the Sun and the Moon, check out these additional resources.

 **Books**

Daley, Michael J. and Buckley Smith. **Amazing Sun Fun Activities.** McGraw-Hill, 1997.

Gardner, Robert. **Science Project Ideas About the Moon.** Enslow, 1997.

Gardner, Robert. **Science Project Ideas About the Sun.** Enslow, 1997.

Moore, Patrick. **The Sun and Moon (The Starry Sky).** Copper Beech Books, 1995.

Nicolson, Cynthia Pratt. **The Moon.** General Distribution Services, 1997.

Organizations and Online Sites

The Exploratorium
3601 Lyon Street
San Francisco, CA 94123
415-397-5673
http://www.exploratorium. edu/science_explorer/ Sunclock.html

This site shows you how to build a Sun clock with just a compass, a pencil, and a diagram that you can print.

American Museum of Natural History
Rose Center for Earth and Space
Central Park West at 79th Street
New York, New York
http://www.amnh.org/rose/ vtours.html

Compare the sizes of the Sun, Moon, Earth, and other planets.

The Franklin Institute Online
The Fels Planetarium
http://sln.fi.edu/tfi/info/fels. html

Find out why the Moon appears larger when it is on the horizon than when it is higher in the sky. Also get some tips for buying a telescope if you want to look at the Moon more closely.

Carnegie Science Center
http://www.carnegie sciencecenter.org/family/ planet_astro.asp

You can find lots of links, including ones with more information about eclipses, sunspots, and how the Moon affects the tides on Earth.

45

Important Words

blue Moon second full Moon that appears in a month

eclipse to block out or cover

ellipse shape that looks like a stretched-out circle

lunar eclipse when Earth blocks the Sun's light from reaching the Moon

parallel being an equal distance apart at every point

shadow dark area made on a surface when something blocks light from reaching it

solar eclipse when the Moon is directly between the Sun and Earth and blocks sunlight from reaching Earth

Index

(**Boldface** page numbers indicate illustrations.)

blue Moon, 23
clock, 33, 34–35
clouds, 5, 6
Copernicus, Nicolaus, 27
darkness, 5, 32
dawn, 22
Earth, 11, **11**, 14, 16, 39
  distance from Sun, 38
  path, 26, 27, 28–30
  travel around Sun, 10, 27, 30, 39
eclipse, 10–11
  lunar, 17, 39
  solar, 11, 14, 39
ellipse, 30, 39
first quarter Moon, 21, **21**
full Moon, 17, 18–31, **22**, 40
gods, **8**
light, 14, 32, 38
lunar eclipse, 17, 39
messages, 41–43
midnight, 21, 22
Moon, 8, 9, 11, **11**, **14**, **17**, 19
  blocking Sun, 12–14, 17, 39
  circling Earth, 10, 39
  full, 17, 18–31, **22**, 40
  fun with, 40–43
  how it disappears, 10–17
  new, 22
  quarters, 21, **21**, 22
moonlight, 40, 42
Morse code, 42–43, **43**
new Moon, 22
noon, 21
planets, 27, 30
quarter Moon, 21, **21**, 22
shadow, 15–17, 31, 32–39
solar eclipse, 10–11, 14, 39
stars, 18, **19**
Sun, 5, 6, 7, 8, 9, **11**, 32
  blocked by Moon, 12–14, 39
  distance from Earth, 38
  fun with, 40–43
  how it disappears, 10–17
  path, 23, 24–26, 27, 30
sundial, **33**
sunlight, 17, 40, 42
sunset, 22
third quarter Moon, 22
three hundred sixty five days, 31, 39
time, 33, 34–35
traveling, 36–38
twenty-four hours, 31
twenty-nine days, 23, 39

Meet the Author

Salvatore Tocci is a science writer who lives in East Hampton, New York, with his wife, Patti. He was a high school biology and chemistry teacher for almost thirty years. As a teacher, he always encouraged his students to perform experiments to learn about science. While surf fishing, he loves watching the Sun rise over the ocean and the full Moon light up the night sky.